CW01072389

Original title:
The Feelings Garden

Author: Penelope Hawthorne
ISBN HARDBACK: 978-9916-88-948-0
ISBN PAPERBACK: 978-9916-88-949-7

The Language of Blossoms

Petals whisper soft and sweet,
In colors bright, they silently greet.
Each bloom tells a tale of the sun,
A moment captured, a life begun.

With fragrance turning heads around,
In gardens where joy can be found.
They speak in hues, in scents so rare,
A silent language, beyond compare.

Nurtured by Time

In gentle hands, the seeds we sow,
To watch them rise, to see them grow.
Day by day, they stretch and reach,
Lessons of patience, time can teach.

Roots sink deep in earth so kind,
Nature's wisdom, intertwined.
Through storms and sun, they brave the day,
Nurtured by time in their own way.

The Dance of Dandelions

Yellow crowns in fields they stand,
A fluttering sea across the land.
With a breeze, they take to flight,
A dance of dreams, a pure delight.

Whispers of wishes on the wind,
In their soft glory, hearts rescind.
Childhood laughter joins the song,
In dandelion's embrace, we belong.

Secrets Beneath the Soil

Beneath the ground, where treasures lie,
In hidden chambers, time drifts by.
Roots entwined in silent grace,
Whispers of life in a dark embrace.

Every grain holds stories old,
Of ancient seeds and dreams retold.
In darkness, life begins to grow,
Secrets beneath the soil we never know.

Nectar of Nostalgia

Memories drip like honey,
Sweet moments lost in time,
Echoes of laughter linger,
Whispers of a simpler rhyme.

Old photos in dusty frames,
Faded smiles, soft delight,
Each glance a gentle flame,
Guiding us through the night.

A scent of lavender blooms,
Take me to the past's embrace,
Where every heart finds room,
In the warmest, safest space.

Yet time carries us away,
Like leaves caught in the breeze,
But the nectar still holds sway,
Bringing sweet moments to seize.

Wildflowers of Yearning

In meadows where dreams run wild,
Colors dance beneath the sun,
Hearts open like flowers, mild,
Searching for the race to be won.

Soft petals whisper secrets,
Of longings hidden deep,
A yearning that never forgets,
In silence, their promises keep.

The evening breeze carries hope,
With blossoms swaying in line,
Through the valleys, we must cope,
For each soul yearns to entwine.

In twilight's gentle embrace,
We wander, lost but found,
Among wildflowers, we trace,
A connection, forever bound.

Seasons of Sorrow

Winter's chill wraps the heart,
With every flake of white,
Memories drift, torn apart,
In the silence of the night.

Spring offers a soft refrain,
A promise of brighter days,
Yet shadows still hold the pain,
In the warmth, a lost gaze.

Summer blazes with its light,
But we feel the aching void,
Beneath the sun, a quiet fight,
As laughter becomes a decoy.

Autumn leaves fall like tears,
Each crinkle a tale unsaid,
Through the passage of the years,
We carry sorrow, thread by thread.

Serenity in the Shade

Beneath the arching trees,
Whispers of nature sway,
Gentle winds bring a breeze,
In the coolness, we lay.

Sunlight dapples the ground,
As shadows softly play,
A hidden peace is found,
In the hush of the day.

Time pauses in this space,
Where worries drift away,
Each heartbeat finds its place,
In the shade, we silently pray.

With moments stitched like seams,
We rest our weary minds,
In this sanctuary of dreams,
True serenity unwinds.

Petals Whispering Wishes

Petals dance on gentle breeze,
Carried far, they softly tease.
Whispers sweet beneath the moon,
Dreams unfurling, hearts in tune.

In the garden, secrets sigh,
Colors blend, a soft goodbye.
Each bloom holds a tale untold,
Hopes and wishes, bright and bold.

Harvesting Memories

Underneath a golden sun,
We gather tales of days well-spun.
Each moment ripe, a treasure found,
In laughter's echo, joy is crowned.

Fields of time, so lush, so vast,
Holding fragments from the past.
Weaving threads of love and light,
In the tapestry of night.

Fertile Ground of Fears

In shadows deep, where anxieties grow,
Roots entwined in thoughts we know.
Tilling soil with trembling hands,
As courage blooms, hope expands.

From darkest nights, new strength we gain,
Through the storms, we learn from pain.
Each tear sown upon the land,
Fuels the fire, helps us stand.

Butterflies of Change

Wings of hues in playful flight,
Transforming day into the night.
In silence, they abandon fear,
Embracing change, they persevere.

Flutter by, the whispers call,
With each change, we rise, we fall.
In the garden of the soul,
Every shift makes us whole.

Seasons of the Soul

In spring, a bud begins to bloom,
Whispers of life dispel the gloom.
Summer dances with radiant light,
Hearts awaken in the warm delight.

Autumn leaves in hues of gold,
Stories of change quietly unfold.
Winter wraps the world in white,
Silence deepens through the night.

Growth Amidst Chaos

In storms of doubt, we learn to stand,
Roots dig deeper in the shifting sand.
Among the wreckage, new dreams ignite,
Hope rises gently, a guiding light.

Fractured paths lead to heights unknown,
From brokenness, a strength has grown.
Chaos swirls, yet we find our way,
Resilient spirits, come what may.

Brush of the Wind

A gentle breeze through emerald trees,
Carries whispers with tender ease.
It paints the skies with a soft caress,
Echoing secrets, nature's finesse.

In meadows wide, it twirls in play,
Guiding the dance of the flowers' sway.
With every gust, a new story spins,
The brush of the wind, where adventure begins.

Colors of Longing

Deep within, desire's flame burns bright,
Painted dreams in the canvas of night.
Scarlet whispers and azure cries,
A palette of hopes beneath starlit skies.

In distant echoes, we hear the call,
A symphony woven for one and all.
Each hue a heartbeat, a wish in flight,
Colors of longing, pure and bright.

Shadowed Corners of Bliss

In quiet nooks where whispers dwell,
Secrets weave their gentle spell.
Soft sunlight filters through the leaves,
In shadowed corners, the heart believes.

Laughter rings like distant chimes,
Echoing through forgotten times.
Moments linger, sweet and rare,
In the hush, we lay our care.

Gentle breezes brush the skin,
Here we find where dreams begin.
In small embraces, joy resides,
In shadowed places, love abides.

Vines of Vulnerability

Twisted tendrils, green and bold,
Climb the heart with stories told.
In fragile frames, we find our place,
Embracing fear with gentle grace.

Layers peel with tender trust,
In open skies, we learn to gust.
Roots entwined beneath the soil,
In shared sunlight, we toil and toil.

Each scar a story, each bruise a sign,
In vulnerability, we intertwine.
Through tangled vines, the blooms will show,
In every risk, our spirits grow.

Colors of the Soul

A canvas bright with hues divine,
Each stroke a whisper, a heartbeat's line.
From deep indigos to fiery red,
In colors true, our truths are said.

Golden sunbeams dance with grace,
In every shade, a sacred space.
Emerald greens, a calming breath,
In vibrant tones, we find our depths.

Brush away the clouds of doubt,
Let rainbows echo, let love shout.
In every color, stories swell,
The soul's rich palette weaves its spell.

The Orchard of Longing

In the orchard, time stands still,
Beneath the boughs, the heart can fill.
Ripened fruits, a tempting sight,
In shadows cast by fading light.

Whispers carried on the breeze,
With each rustle, a silent tease.
Branches heavy with dreams untold,
In every longing, a story unfolds.

Footsteps trace the winding ground,
In this haven, peace is found.
The harvest waits, a bittersweet,
In the orchard, heart and hope meet.

Fragrance of Forgotten Dreams

In the quiet of the night,
Whispers of old hopes rise,
Carried on the gentle breeze,
A scent that never dies.

Memories wrapped in twilight,
Echoes of laughter's song,
Fading like the starlit sky,
Yet somehow feeling strong.

They linger in the shadows,
Like petals on the ground,
Their essence paints the silence,
A beauty lost, yet found.

Awake to find the echoes,
In dreams that softly bloom,
Fragrance of forgotten nights,
Still breathing in the room.

Seedlings of Hope

In the soil of our hearts,
Tiny seeds start to grow,
Nurtured by the light of dreams,
In the sun's warm glow.

Each tender sprout a promise,
Reaching for the skies,
Whispers of tomorrow,
In every green surprise.

Through storms and gentle rains,
They learn to stand up tall,
With roots that dig in deeper,
They'll never fade at all.

So let the garden flourish,
In the heart where hope is sown,
For every seed that's nurtured,
Will find its way back home.

Budding Tenderness

In the warmth of soft embraces,
Love begins to bloom,
Petals open slowly,
Filling hearts with room.

A touch of gentle kindness,
A smile that warms the day,
In the dance of budding hearts,
Tender words can say.

Like flowers reaching upward,
In the sunlight's kiss,
Each moment shared together,
Is a chance not to miss.

So nurture this connection,
Let it sprout and grow,
For in life's vibrant garden,
Love's the seed we sow.

Raindrops on Heartstrings

Softly falling memories,
As raindrops touch the ground,
Each one sings a story,
A melody profound.

They dance upon the rooftops,
In a gentle, rhythmic grace,
Creating tunes of longing,
In this sacred place.

With every drop that whispers,
A tear of joy or pain,
The heartstrings start to tremble,
In the sweet, soft rain.

So let the droplets gather,
In puddles deep and wide,
For every raindrop's echo,
Holds love that will abide.

Enchanted Conversations

Whispers dance between the trees,
Tales of old float on the breeze.
Secrets linger in the night,
Stars above, a guiding light.

Voices echo in the dark,
Each word a shimmering spark.
In the twilight, hearts unite,
In the stillness, dreams take flight.

Murmurs weave through moonlit glades,
Where sincerity never fades.
With each glance, a story shared,
In this moment, love declared.

Blossom of Yesterdays

Petals fall like whispered dreams,
Fading memories, or so it seems.
Once vibrant hues of laughter bright,
Now softened by the gentle night.

Time's embrace, a fragrant breeze,
Echoes stir beneath the trees.
In the garden of our past,
Blooming moments meant to last.

Tangled roots of joy and pain,
Rain or shine, they bloom again.
From the soil of what we've known,
New blossoms from the seeds we've sown.

Sprouting Serenity

In the hush of morning light,
Softly comes a peaceful sight.
Gentle greens begin to rise,
Nature's calm beneath the skies.

Leaves unfurl like whispered grace,
In each bud, a sacred space.
Quiet moments, deep and real,
In this stillness, hearts can heal.

Roots entwined beneath the ground,
Where tranquility is found.
Time stands still as life unfolds,
In the quiet, joy beholds.

The Heart's Canopy

Underneath the woven leaves,
Sheltered from what time conceives.
Whispers of a serene song,
In the shade, we both belong.

Branches stretch, a living dome,
In this magic, we feel home.
Every heartbeat, every breath,
Underneath this shield from death.

Sunlight dapples on the ground,
In this haven, love is found.
With each sigh, the world's embraced,
In the heart's canopy, we're graced.

Emotions in Full Blossom

In the garden of my heart,
Feelings bloom like flowers bright,
Joy and sorrow intertwined,
Colors dance in morning light.

Whispers of love fill the air,
Petals soft, a gentle touch,
Memories linger, sweet and rare,
Through the thorns, we feel so much.

Each tear a dew drop freshly shed,
Every laugh a sunlit ray,
Together in this life we tread,
In the garden, come what may.

As seasons shift and petals fall,
Roots grow deep beneath the ground,
In our hearts, we hear their call,
Emotions' beauty knows no bounds.

A Tapestry of Tenderness

In threads of love we weave,
A story soft and warm,
With every hug, we believe,
In the shelter of our charm.

Moments stitched with care and grace,
Patterns of laughter intertwined,
In this safe and sacred space,
Our hearts forever aligned.

Gentle words, like silk, caress,
Binding us in sweet surrender,
Through trials, we learn to bless,
Every heartbeat, a reminder.

Together we write this song,
Each note a promise, pure and true,
In this tapestry, we belong,
A love that always renews.

Sunlight Through the Leaves

Golden rays break through the boughs,
Kissing earth with warmth and light,
Nature's whispers, soft and low,
Guide our hearts to take flight.

The rustling leaves sing sweetly,
Stories of a time gone by,
In their shade, we feel complete,
As the world spins in the sky.

Each beam a promise, bright and clear,
Chasing shadows, filling space,
In this moment, we draw near,
To each other's warm embrace.

Sunset hues paint vast horizons,
Merging day and night divine,
In our hearts, a spark ignites,
A love that forever shines.

Thorns of Joy and Sorrow

In a garden of mixed blooms,
Joy and sorrow coexist,
Thorns protect what love consumes,
In each heart, a tender twist.

We learn to cherish every prick,
For beauty lies in bittersweet,
With every laugh and every kick,
Life's a dance, a trick, a feat.

Holding close the hearts we share,
Through the pain, we find our way,
With each thorn, a lesson fair,
Guiding us to brighter days.

So let us wander, hand in hand,
Through this wild and wooly place,
For in thorns, we understand,
The depth of love's embrace.

Sunlit Aspirations

In morning light, dreams take flight,
Soft whispers call, hearts feel bright.
With every step, the path unfolds,
A journey made of hopes and gold.

Clouds may loom, but hope will stay,
Guiding us through the light of day.
With open hearts, we chase the sun,
Aspirations bright, we will outrun.

Gentle breezes, a soothing song,
In unity, we all belong.
Together we rise, hand in hand,
In sunlit fields, forever we stand.

Through trials faced, we stand our ground,
In every shadow, light is found.
Embrace the dawn, let spirits soar,
In sunlit dreams, forevermore.

Roots of Regret

In the quiet of night, echoes stir,
Memories clash, feelings blur.
Paths once chosen, now entangled,
In the shadows, old dreams tangled.

Whispers of choices haunt the mind,
Regrets like vines, tightly bind.
A fading hope lost in the past,
Wishing for moments that couldn't last.

Yet in the dark, a spark remains,
Lessons learned through all the pains.
From the ashes, new roots can grow,
Embracing wounds, letting them show.

With every tear, we find the light,
Transforming sorrow into flight.
For even in darkness, seeds are sown,
From roots of regret, new strength is grown.

Blossoms of Joy

In gardens lush, colors embrace,
Sunlit petals, a warm grace.
Laughter dances on gentle air,
In blossoms bright, joy is laid bare.

With every bloom, hope takes its stand,
Nature's canvas, divinely planned.
Sweet fragrances fill the day,
In every heart, joy finds a way.

Children play in fields so wide,
Chasing dreams, hearts open wide.
The world awakens, eyes aglow,
In the warmth of summer's flow.

Together we savor life's sweet song,
In every moment, we all belong.
With open arms, let love deploy,
In every heart, find blossoms of joy.

Secrets in the Soil

Beneath the earth, whispers reside,
Stories buried, secrets hide.
Roots entwined with ancient lore,
In the soil, dreams to explore.

Life's tapestry weaves through time,
Echoes of nature, a silent rhyme.
Nurtured whispers touch the heart,
In the shadows, life takes part.

Seasons change, yet still they keep,
In their embrace, a promise deep.
From winter's chill to summer's grace,
Secrets flourish, time won't erase.

Listen close and you will find,
In the soil, we're intertwined.
Each secret shared, a bond unfolds,
In nature's arms, the truth is told.

Serendipity Amongst Stems

In a garden where secrets bloom,
Colors dance amidst the gloom,
Every stem a hidden tale,
Whispers carried on a gentle gale.

Beneath the sun's soft, golden rays,
Life emerges in wondrous ways,
Petals flutter, hearts take flight,
In this haven, pure delight.

Each encounter, a sweet surprise,
Bringing forth joy in disguise,
Nature's brush paints the scene,
In this moment, we feel serene.

Here in the weave of time and space,
Every flower finds its place,
Amongst the stems, life feels vast,
In serendipity, we're steadfast.

The Unfurled Heart

Once a bud, so tightly bound,
Hidden thoughts within, profound,
Time, the gentle hand of fate,
Opens petals, love's innate.

In the breeze, it starts to sway,
Reaching out, with hopes to play,
Each color speaks of dreams anew,
The unfurled heart seeks its due.

Sunlight bathes the tender bloom,
In its warmth, fears find no room,
In the silence, love will sing,
To the unspoken, life takes wing.

Let the world come closer now,
In this moment, we make a vow,
To nurture hope, to never part,
In the beauty of the unfurled heart.

A Field of Longing

Beneath the sky, a sea of green,
Whispers of dreams remain unseen,
Each blade of grass, a wish untold,
In this field, hearts unfold.

With each breeze, a sigh escapes,
Echoes linger, a world that shapes,
Longing dances in the light,
In this vastness, hearts ignite.

Footsteps trace the paths we knew,
Every second feels so new,
In the shadows, hope takes root,
In a field of longing, dreams are brute.

Underneath the stars' soft gaze,
We find solace in the haze,
In the quiet, our dreams collide,
In this field, we cannot hide.

Echoes of Sunflowers

In fields where sunflowers turn their face,
Golden orbs in a warm embrace,
Each petal captures tales of light,
Echoes linger, day turns to night.

Beneath the sun, they stand so tall,
Reaching high, embracing all,
Whispers of love in the breeze,
Every sway puts our hearts at ease.

In their gaze, the world feels bright,
A dance of shadows, a splash of light,
With every bloom, hope softly glows,
Echoing joy, as the heart knows.

As dusk descends, the colors fade,
Yet in each heart, memories stayed,
Echoes of sunflowers, pure and free,
In their presence, we all long to be.

Fragrance of Forgotten Joys

In the garden where laughter grew,
Petals whisper of days anew.
Sunshine softened the evening light,
Memories linger, bold and bright.

Time's gentle hands have brushed away,
The colors of a yesterday.
Yet in the breeze, I catch a trace,
Of joy that time cannot erase.

Each scent that dances through the air,
Brings tales of love and tender care.
A hint of sweetness, soft and light,
Reminds me of those carefree nights.

So let me bask in moments past,
Where echoes of my heart hold fast.
In fragrant blooms, I'll find my way,
To cherish joys that always stay.

Unfurling Layers of Heart

Beneath the surface, still and deep,
Lie secrets that my heart must keep.
With every layer, stories trace,
The essence of my tender space.

In gentle whispers, truths emerge,
With every pulse, sensations surge.
Peeling back the burdens, light,
Reveals the beauty in the fight.

An open heart, a trusting touch,
Invites the world, it's never too much.
Unfurling like the morning dew,
Each layer speaks, clear and true.

I find my strength in what I share,
The woven threads of love and care.
In vulnerabilities, we thrive,
A symphony of hearts alive.

Roots of Resilience

Deep in the soil, where shadows play,
Roots intertwine, holding sway.
Strength emerges from silent ground,
In every whisper, hope is found.

Through storms that rage and winds that howl,
A firm foundation will not cowl.
With every challenge, deeper they spread,
Anchoring dreams that lie ahead.

In nurturing earth, though life may bend,
The spirit rises, fierce to mend.
We draw our power from the strife,
In every struggle, blooms new life.

So let them grow, those roots so wide,
In strength and grace, we shall abide.
For through the trials, we do find,
The roots of resilience, intertwined.

Dance of the Daisies

On meadows bright, where daisies sway,
A cheerful dance at end of day.
With every breeze, they rise and twirl,
In playful steps, they spin and whirl.

Each white petal, a smile they share,
In sunlight's glow, beyond compare.
They nod to clouds, that drift above,
A dance of joy, a song of love.

As shadows lengthen, colors blend,
The daisies twine, and laughter bends.
A symphony of nature's grace,
In harmony, they find their place.

So join the dance, let spirits soar,
With every step, we're wanting more.
In circles wide, let hearts be free,
In the dance of daisies, you and me.

Gentle Breezes of Hope

Whispers of the morning light,
Easing sorrows, taking flight.
Softly sways the willow tree,
Promises of what can be.

Carried on the fragrant air,
Dreams are born without a care.
Fluttering petals, bright and fair,
Hearts awakened, love to share.

In the hush of evening's glow,
Breezes bring a sense of flow.
Tales of joy and peace they weave,
In the night, we dare to believe.

With each sigh, a spark ignites,
Guiding us through shadowed nights.
Gentle breezes softly sing,
Hope, a gentle, sacred thing.

A Symphony of Colors

Brushstrokes dance across the sky,
Crimson, gold, as day waves bye.
Nature's canvas, broad and wide,
In every hue, our dreams abide.

Emerald fields where daisies bloom,
Tangerine sunsets chase the gloom.
Lapis lakes reflect the stars,
A vibrant heart, our healing scars.

Lavender sighs in twilight's peace,
In the colors, sorrows cease.
A symphony, each shade a note,
Life in harmony does float.

Each petal, leaf, and grain of sand,
Forms a beauty, hand in hand.
Together we will paint the scene,
A masterpiece, forever green.

Echoes Beneath the Leaves

Rustling whispers, secrets shared,
Nature's stories, unprepar'd.
Footsteps echo, soft and light,
Beneath the leaves, hearts take flight.

Sheltered by the ancient trees,
Melodies ride the gentle breeze.
In the shadows, laughter plays,
Echoes of our golden days.

Sunlight filters through the boughs,
On life's journey, here and now.
Every rustle speaks a truth,
In the woods, we find our youth.

Listen close, hear nature's call,
Echoes of love surround us all.
Beneath the leaves, our spirits soar,
In the quiet, we explore.

Midnight Lavender Dreams

In the stillness of the night,
Lavender scents take their flight.
Whispers float on silken air,
Drifting softly, without a care.

Stars that twinkle, so serene,
In this world, we weave a scene.
Moonlight bathes the quiet land,
Holding dreams in a gentle hand.

Night unfolds its velvet cloak,
Every thought is softly spoke.
Dancing shadows, dreams take shape,
In this realm, there's no escape.

As the dawn begins to break,
Lavender echoes, sweet awake.
Midnight whispers fade away,
Yet in dreams, we'll always stay.

Glistening Dewdrops of Dawn

As dawn breaks with a gentle hue,
Dewdrops glisten on leaves anew.
Nature awakens from night's calm hold,
Each droplet tells a story untold.

Sunrise paints the world so bright,
Colors burst, a pure delight.
Birds sing sweetly, a morning song,
In this moment, we all belong.

Whispers of light kiss the grass,
Each glimmering drop, a fleeting pass.
Time stands still, in this soft glow,
As dewdrops dance, as breezes flow.

Echoes of Unspoken Words.

In shadows linger thoughts unsaid,
Echoes of love or fear instead.
Silent glances fill the air,
Words unspoken, a heavy fare.

Each heartbeat thunders like a drum,
In quiet rooms where whispers come.
A gaze that lingers, a breath held tight,
Promises made in the fading light.

In dreams we speak, in silence we feel,
A hidden truth that time can heal.
With every pause, our hearts unfold,
Life's greatest stories left untold.

Whispers of Petals

Soft petals fall from trees of grace,
Each one dances with elegant pace.
Nature's confetti, a fragrant show,
Carried by breezes, where memories flow.

In gardens where colors unite,
The whispers of petals, a sweet delight.
Fragrance lingers, so soft and pure,
In every bloom, a love to endure.

Underneath the vast blue sky,
Petals hold secrets, they flutter by.
With every whisper, a story we share,
In the hush of moments, floating in air.

Echoes in Bloom

In fields where the wildflowers play,
Echoes in bloom light up the day.
Colors weave in a vibrant dance,
Nature's canvas, a fleeting chance.

Bees hum softly, gathering fate,
In each blossom, a love innate.
Sunlight kisses the petals wide,
Mirroring the joy we can't hide.

With every breeze, a story takes flight,
Reminders of beauty in gentle light.
In each fleeting moment, we find our way,
Echoes in bloom, forever stay.

Whispers of the Wind

Through the trees, the whispers flow,
Secrets soft, in breezes grow.
Carrying tales from far away,
In the dusk, they softly sway.

Listen close, the murmurs blend,
Nature speaks, our silent friend.
Winds may dance, or gently sigh,
In their song, we learn to fly.

With each gust, a story clears,
Echoes of both hopes and fears.
In the stillness, we can find,
The hidden voice that stirs the mind.

So let the wind, with soft embrace,
Guide our steps to sacred space.
Together with its tender hum,
We'll unravel where we're from.

The Garden Within

In the quiet of the soul,
Seeds of dreams begin to roll.
Watered by our hopes and tears,
Nurtured through the passing years.

Petals bloom in vibrant hue,
Each a wish, both bold and true.
In the garden, hearts are free,
Growing wide with empathy.

Weeds may come and shadows fall,
Yet we cherish through it all.
Digging deep, we learn to sow,
Love and kindness help us grow.

Fruits of joy found in our hearts,
Harvested through all our parts.
In this space of peace and light,
The garden thrives, a pure delight.

Roots and Wings

From the earth, our roots extend,
Grounded deep, where journeys blend.
Nurtured by the love we share,
Strengthened through the bonds we bear.

With each branch, we reach for skies,
Wings spread wide, we learn to rise.
Soaring high, yet tied to ground,
In this balance, life is found.

Storms may shake, and winds may roar,
But the roots hold, forevermore.
In the dance of earth and air,
We discover what we dare.

As we fly, we still can see,
The strength in roots, the joy of free.
Together, they form our song,
Roots and wings, where we belong.

Shadows Under Canopies

Beneath the trees, a whisper glows,
Dancing leaves as soft wind blows.
Echoes hide in dappled light,
Secrets shared by day and night.

Shadows stretch like eager hands,
Tracing patterns on the sands.
Nature's quilt, a gentle weave,
In every space, the heart believes.

Harvest of Memories

Fields of gold where stories grow,
Time entwines in ebb and flow.
Every grain, a moment's grace,
Tells the tale of a loved face.

Seasons shift, yet still we keep,
In our hearts, those memories seep.
Each recall, a vibrant hue,
A harvest rich, forever true.

Blooming in Silence

Petals open, none can see,
Beauty blooms in quiet glee.
Gentle fragrance fills the air,
Whispers soft, beyond compare.

In the stillness, life takes flight,
Colors dance in muted light.
Growth unseen, yet full of might,
A vibrant world hidden from sight.

Roots of Resilience

Deep underground, the roots entwine,
Strength and hope in each design.
Against the storms, they stand so strong,
Holding on where they belong.

Seasons change, yet they persist,
Nurtured dreams that still exist.
From the earth, their courage wakes,
In every trial, the spirit breaks.

Reflections in the Rain

Puddles gather in the light,
Mirroring clouds, a somber sight.
Droplets dance upon the ground,
Whispers of silence all around.

Each ripple tells a muted tale,
As shadows flicker, soft and pale.
Rainy hues in gray delight,
Emotions wash in pure respite.

Windows streak with memories bright,
In each droplet, dreams take flight.
Nature's brush on canvas wet,
In the rain, all fears forget.

So let the storm pour out the night,
Cleansing hearts with gentle might.
In reflections, peace is found,
As raindrops sing, a soothing sound.

Petal by Petal

Blossoms open, shades of grace,
Nature's jewels in a warm embrace.
Petals flutter with the breeze,
Whispering secrets through the trees.

Colors painted in the sun,
Each flower holds a world begun.
Beauty unfolds, a timeless show,
In gardens where soft breezes blow.

Delicate scents fill the air,
Inviting hearts to linger there.
Petal by petal, life reveals,
Magic held in what it feels.

In every bloom, a story told,
A fleeting moment to behold.
Nature's canvas, ever bright,
Petal by petal, pure delight.

Lingering Aromas

Spices dance upon the stove,
Cinnamon dreams in the air weave.
Coffee brews with morning's light,
Lingering aromas, a sweet invite.

Herbs whisper tales from the past,
Of kitchens warm and friendships vast.
Each scent a memory to cling,
In the heart, their joy will sing.

The fragrance of rain on earth,
Awakens souls with gentle mirth.
In each breath, the world unfolds,
Lingering aromas, stories told.

As seasons change, the scents may fade,
Yet in our hearts, they still invade.
Toast to flavors, rich and warm,
Lingering aromas, a lasting charm.

Tides of Emotion

Waves crash softly on the shore,
Emotions swell, then they bore.
With every rise, a heart will break,
Fleeting moments we cannot shake.

The moon pulls tightly on the sea,
Guiding feelings wild and free.
In the depths, shadows collide,
Tides of sorrow, love's sweet ride.

Each ebb and flow, a journey traced,
In watery paths, our hopes embraced.
The ocean's roar, the quiet sighs,
In tides of emotion, truth complies.

So let the waters hold you near,
As waves of doubt begin to clear.
Feel the rhythm, strong and bold,
In tides of emotion, stories unfold.

Whispers Among the Petals

In gardens where the soft winds play,
The petals dance at close of day.
Each whisper shared, a secret told,
In colors bright, a tale unfolds.

The bees hum tunes of sweet delight,
As twilight paints the world in light.
Among the blooms, a fleeting sigh,
Where dreams take wing and gently fly.

A breeze carries a fragrant tune,
Beneath the gaze of the silver moon.
Each petal holds a promise dear,
In whispers, love draws ever near.

And as the stars begin to gleam,
The flowers weave a tender dream.
In every rustle, a heart's refrain,
Whispers of joy, born from the rain.

Blooms of Solitude

In shadows deep, where silence reigns,
The blooms of solitude break chains.
With petals soft and colors bright,
They stand alone, a wondrous sight.

The evening air, a gentle sigh,
As lonely hearts begin to cry.
Yet in each bloom, a story swells,
Of strength found in the quiet spells.

They whisper tales of battles fought,
In the solitude, wisdom sought.
Rooted firm in untouched earth,
Each bloom conveys a sense of worth.

So let the petals softly fall,
In solitude, we hear the call.
Within the stillness, courage grows,
In blooms of solitude, love shows.

Thorns of Tomorrow

In gardens where the dark blooms grow,
A tale of thorns begins to show.
They hold a beauty, sharp and bright,
A lesson learned in darkest night.

Each thorn a mark of battles won,
A testimony to the sun.
For every bloom that seeks the sky,
The thorns remind us why we try.

In moments when the heart feels cold,
The thorns reveal the strength of soul.
They tell of struggles, strife, and pain,
Yet in their grip, we break the chain.

So when you see the flowers rise,
Remember well the thorns that lie.
For tomorrow's blooms, resilient, bold,
Are forged by thorns, as life unfolds.

Raindrops of Reflection

Beneath the clouds, the world awakes,
With raindrops falling, nature quakes.
Each droplet mirrors skies of gray,
In puddles deep, our dreams will sway.

The whispers rain upon my face,
Each drop a moment, a soft embrace.
They shimmer like the thoughts we mold,
Reflections of the stories told.

In every splash, a memory wakes,
Life's rhythm flows, as thunder shakes.
Through storms we find the peace we seek,
In raindrops' dance, our spirits speak.

So let the rain fall free and wild,
It nurtures earth, it soothes the child.
With every drop, a chance to grow,
In raindrops of reflection, love will flow.

A Symphony of Senses

The sight of dawn paints gold in the sky,
A whisper of wind, a soft lullaby.
The taste of sweetness on lips intertwined,
Harmony found in each breath entined.

Notes of laughter dance through the air,
Touch of a hand, a moment to share.
The scent of blossoms, fresh and alive,
In this symphony, our spirits thrive.

Sound of the rain, a gentle embrace,
Melody of life, in each quiet space.
Bringing together, the world sings soft,
In this symphony, our souls lift aloft.

All senses awaken, wrapped in this light,
Together we bask in the warmest night.
With every heartbeat, a rhythm so true,
In this grand orchestra, it's me and you.

Butterfly Kisses

A flutter of wings, so delicate, bright,
Whispers of love in the soft morning light.
Gentle embrace in the garden of dreams,
Where time loses track, and all is as it seems.

The brush of a wing, a tender caress,
Moments of magic, we quietly bless.
Each flicker of color, a story to tell,
In the dance of the butterflies, our hearts dwell.

In flowers we find, a haven of bliss,
Kisses like petals, no moment to miss.
With laughter and joy, we twirl through the day,
Like butterfly kisses, we drift and we sway.

Together we wander, in gardens so fair,
Finding our peace in the sweet scented air.
A journey of love, forever unfolds,
In these butterfly kisses, a story unfolds.

The Aroma of Affection

The scent of the morning, warm and inviting,
Coffee and spices, the world igniting.
With every aroma, memories bloom,
Wrapped in the warmth, a soft fragrant room.

Baking of bread, a delicious embrace,
The taste of your laughter, I long to retrace.
Candles softly flicker, their fragrance divine,
In this cozy haven, your heart, it is mine.

The spice of affection, in whispers it grows,
Entwined together, like vines, love knows.
With each gentle breeze, your essence I feel,
In the aroma of love, our hearts gently heal.

In every moment, the senses align,
Savoring sweetness, our spirits entwined.
The fragrance of memories, rich as a song,
In this aroma of affection, we forever belong.

Stirrings of the Heart

In twilight's embrace, emotions arise,
A whisper of hope in the star-studded skies.
With each fleeting glance, a spark ignites,
The stirrings of heart in the still of the nights.

A soft touch of hand, a gaze that connects,
With every heartbeat, our love it reflects.
The warmth of your smile, a beacon of light,
Guiding my soul through the depths of the night.

Each moment together, a dance we create,
Our spirits take flight, as we navigate fate.
In the stillness of breath, we softly confide,
The stirrings of heart, in this beautiful ride.

In whispers of dreams, we find our own way,
Through the ebb and the flow, come what may.
In the journey of us, where true love imparts,
Forever entwined are the stirrings of hearts.

Vines of Vulnerability

In the garden, shadows play,
Where the soft blooms sway.
Beneath their tender grace,
Lie stories we embrace.

Fingers trace the tangled roots,
Dancing lightly in their suits.
Each vine a fragile tale,
Of strength that will prevail.

Whispers echo through the leaves,
Secrets held that never grieves.
Through the storms they intertwine,
Their beauty is divine.

So let us grow, entwined as one,
In the glow of moon and sun.
For in the stretch of every climb,
We find our love through space and time.

Petals Underfoot

Upon the ground, soft petals lay,
Colorful reminders of yesterday.
Each hue a memory held tight,
Whispering secrets in the light.

Footsteps dance through nature's grace,
As petals brush against our face.
With every crunch beneath our tread,
The stories of the past we're fed.

In the fleeting joy of spring,
Life's simple pleasures they do bring.
These fragments of a moment's bloom,
Radiate warmth, dispel the gloom.

Let us treasure what we find,
In the petals that entwine.
For as they scatter in the breeze,
Their beauty lingers, hearts at ease.

The Whispering Breeze

A gentle breath upon my skin,
Where day begins and dreams begin.
It carries tales of distant lands,
And brushes softly through our hands.

In the quiet hush of night,
The breeze speaks low, a soft delight.
It weaves through trees, and stirs the night,
Revealing visions, pure and bright.

With every gust, new secrets told,
In whispers soft, both brave and bold.
It wraps around with tender grace,
A calming touch we all embrace.

So let the whispers fill the air,
With dreams and hopes beyond compare.
For in the breeze, we find our peace,
A breath of life that will not cease.

Thorns and Tenderness

In a garden, sharp and fine,
Thorns protect what is divine.
Amidst the danger, beauty grows,
In the heart, a warmth that flows.

A tender hand can feel the sting,
Yet binds us close, as if a string.
For every wound, there lies a grace,
A love that time cannot erase.

Through trials faced and battles won,
The heart's resilient under sun.
Thorns may pierce, but love will mend,
In this dance, we rise and blend.

So cherish thorns, embrace the pain,
For in the storm, there is refrain.
Together, in this tangled dance,
We find our strength, our true romance.

Nourished by Kindness

In warm embraces, hearts align,
Gentle words like soft sunshine.
Lifting souls when shadows creep,
In kindness, promises we keep.

A smile shared, a hand to hold,
In silent gestures, love unfolds.
Through stormy days, we find the light,
In every act, our spirits bright.

Nurtured by the love we show,
Seeds of hope begin to grow.
Together, we can change the tide,
With kindness, we shall abide.

Let kindness bloom, as flowers rise,
In every heart, beneath the skies.
For in this world, so vast and wide,
It's love and care that truly guide.

Sunsets and Silhouettes

The sun dips low, the sky ablaze,
Colors dance in evening's haze.
Silhouettes against the glow,
A fleeting moment, soft and slow.

Whispers of daylight fade away,
Nighttime's charm begins to play.
Painting dreams on twilight's breath,
In this beauty, we forget death.

Stars peek through the velvet dark,
Guiding dreams with a tiny spark.
Every sunset tells a tale,
Of love, of loss, of the grand scale.

In every hue, a memory,
Of laughter shared, of joy set free.
Sunsets and silhouettes, they blend,
A canvas where our hearts can mend.

Silent Whispers of Nature

In rustling leaves, a secret sigh,
Nature speaks as time drifts by.
Mountains echo soft, sweet calls,
A symphony in crystal halls.

Beneath the stars, the night reveals,
The world spins slow, our hearts it heals.
In gentle streams, the water flows,
Tales of life in murmurs show.

Birds take flight in dawn's embrace,
While wildflowers dance with grace.
Every corner, peace is found,
In nature's arms, we are unbound.

Silent whispers, earthy tones,
In solitude, we find our own.
Listening deep, a calming balm,
In every breath, we find the calm.

Heartbeats in Bloom

In springtime's glow, our spirits rise,
With every petal, hope defies.
Heartbeats thrumming, life anew,
In vibrant colors, dreams break through.

Life's tender touch, a warm refrain,
In garden paths, we lose our pain.
Each bloom a tale, a love expanded,
In nature's arms, our souls have landed.

When shadows fall and doubts creep in,
Nature's beauty reigns within.
In every heartbeat, life's sweet tune,
Whispers softly of the moon.

Together we dance, hearts in sync,
As blossoms open, we will think.
Through every season, love will thrive,
In heartbeats, we feel alive.

Fragments of Joy

In laughter's echo, shadows play,
Moments wrapped in bright array.
A fleeting glance, a warm embrace,
In fleeting time, I find my place.

The sunlit dance on leaves of green,
In tiny sparks, my heart's unseen.
With every heartbeat, love's reply,
I gather all these fragments, nigh.

In sweet reminders, memories bloom,
A tapestry of light from gloom.
Each little joy, a world to hold,
In tender tales, my heart unfolds.

Through whispered winds, and soft moonlight,
I chase the dreams that spark the night.
In every dawn, a brand-new start,
These fragments linger in my heart.

The Soil of Solitude

In quiet corners of my mind,
The roots of thought are intertwined.
Beneath the surface, seeds take flight,
In silence blooms a world of light.

Lonely paths, yet oh so clear,
In solitude, I shed my fear.
With every breath, the earth's embrace,
I find my peace, my hidden place.

The whispers of the evening breeze,
Invite my heart to bend with ease.
In solitude's vast, fertile land,
I cultivate what I have planned.

From stillness grows a sacred tree,
A monument to what can be.
In every leaf, a story told,
Of strength reclaimed and dreams of old.

Awakening in Color

A canvas blank, the morning breaks,
With hues of warmth, the silence shakes.
In vivid strokes, the day unfolds,
A symphony of bright and bold.

The flowers bloom in radiant cheer,
Each petal holds a memory dear.
Where once was gray, now life ignites,
Awakening in vibrant sights.

The sky, a palette, vast and wide,
In every tone, the dreams abide.
With every shade, a promise new,
Awakening, I feel it too.

In sunset's glow, I find my way,
Through colors that can never sway.
A brush of wonder paints my soul,
Awakening in beauty whole.

Cherished Roots

In ancient soil, my story weaves,
Beneath the boughs where sunlight leaves.
With whispered tales of yesteryear,
The roots of love forever near.

Through storms and calm, they anchor deep,
In corners of my heart, they keep.
A tapestry of loss and gain,
Cherished roots, through joy and pain.

The branches stretch, in search of skies,
And every glance, a sweet reprise.
With every season, life renews,
In cherished roots, my strength ensues.

From humble start, I rise and grow,
A legacy, my heart can show.
In every leaf, a memory,
Cherished roots, forever free.

Blooming Resilience

In cracks of stone, flowers grow,
A testament to strength, they show.
With every storm, their roots hold tight,
They rise again, embracing light.

Through trials fierce and skies of gray,
They bend but do not break away.
With colors bright, they face the day,
A dance of life in bold display.

In gardens wild, they find their place,
Resilience blooms with silent grace.
Through shadows long, they seek the sun,
In every heart, their hope's begun.

With gentle whispers, winds still blow,
Each petal tells the tales we know.
In unity, they proudly stand,
Together stronger, hand in hand.

A Harvest of Dreams

In fields of gold where wishes grow,
Beneath the skies, their blessings flow.
Each star above, a dream untold,
In moonlit nights, their stories unfold.

With every seed, intentions thrive,
In whispered hopes, they come alive.
Through seasons long, we tend with care,
The garden of dreams that we all share.

When autumn comes, we gather near,
The fruits of faith, each one is dear.
In woven paths, our spirits gleam,
Together we reap this harvest dream.

With laughter shared and hands entwined,
In unity, our hearts combined.
Through trials faced, our love supreme,
We celebrate this precious dream.

Shadows and Sunbeams

In the embrace of dusk and dawn,
Where shadows dance and light is drawn.
Each fleeting moment, soft and fast,
A fleeting glance, too soon it's past.

With sunlit smiles and whispers low,
The world transforms in golden glow.
Yet shadows linger, ever near,
Reminders of both hope and fear.

In twilight's grace, we find our way,
Through paths of light, we learn to stay.
In harmony, the worlds align,
With shadows cast, our souls can shine.

Embracing night, we're not alone,
In every heart, a light has grown.
Through dark and bright, we learn to see,
The beauty found in you and me.

Thickets of Emotion

Within the woods where feelings hide,
In tangled vines, the heart confides.
Each leaf unfurls, a hope revealed,
In thickets deep, our wounds are healed.

With rustling leaves, the whispers sway,
Through tangled paths, we find our way.
In every thorn, a lesson learned,
In every bend, a passion burned.

From joy to pain, the range is vast,
In shadows long, we face the past.
Yet through the thickets, we grow wise,
Discovering truth behind the skies.

In nature's hands, our stories blend,
Through every twist, we make amends.
With strength in roots and hearts entwined,
In thickets deep, our souls aligned.

Reflection in Dew Drops

Morning light on blades of grass,
Each dew drop holds a past.
Whispers of the night's embrace,
Glimmers soft in nature's space.

In their round, the world reflects,
Dreams and hopes, the heart connects.
Nature's jewels, delicate, true,
Moments caught, both fresh and new.

With each breath, the day awakes,
In the stillness, silence breaks.
Glistening orbs, like time stood still,
Carrying whispers from the hill.

As the sun climbs ever high,
Dew drops fade into the sky.
Yet the memory will stay,
In the heart, a bright bouquet.

Harmony Amongst Weeds

In the garden, life can thrive,
Weeds and blooms, all come alive.
Colors clash but find a way,
To blend in beauty's gentle sway.

Amongst the thorns and tangled green,
A symphony, though rarely seen.
Each petal and each leaf that bends,
In nature's dance, all are friends.

Voices rise in the evening light,
Nature's chorus, pure delight.
Every creature plays its part,
Together, they fill up the heart.

So let us learn from weeds and flowers,
Harmony in all our hours.
For in the chaos, there exists,
A bond that nature truly kissed.

Unraveled Vines

Twisting upward towards the sun,
Vines entwined, their journey begun.
Through the shadow, through the light,
Striving onward, taking flight.

Strength in each unfurling leaf,
Holding on through joy and grief.
In their paths, a story weaves,
Tales of hope in gentle leaves.

With every climb, a challenge met,
Never yielding, no regret.
Nature's will, so wild and free,
Unraveled hearts to simply be.

Embrace the growth, let love entwine,
Find your path, like those bold vines.
In the dance of life's design,
Be the strength that intertwines.

Bloom Where You're Planted

In a pot, or in the field,
Every seed has strength concealed.
Though the soil may seem unkind,
Beauty waits for you to find.

With sunlight's touch and gentle rain,
Each new day brings forth the gain.
Roots may twist but still they grow,
In every challenge, beauty shows.

Spread your petals, let them shine,
Be your own, for you are divine.
No matter where your journey starts,
Every bloom, a work of art.

So bloom in grace, with colors bright,
Radiate your truest light.
Embrace the gifts that life has planned,
And bloom where you are planted.

Petals of Memory

In the meadow where we danced,
The blossoms whisper secrets vast.
Colors fade like soft romance,
Each petal holds a moment passed.

Sunny days and laughter clear,
Echoes linger in the breeze.
Time holds still, yet I hold dear,
These fleeting joys like summer leaves.

Beneath the boughs where shadows play,
We carved our names in bark so deep.
Years may fold and drift away,
Yet in my heart, our promises keep.

So let the petals fall like rain,
Each whisper brings you back to me.
In every tinge of joy and pain,
Your memory blooms eternally.

Garden of Reflection

In the quiet of the night,
Stars adorn the velvet sky,
Each one shines a guiding light,
Inviting dreams as they fly by.

Footpaths lined with fragrant blooms,
Whispers dance on twilight air.
In the stillness, wisdom looms,
Nature's heart laid slightly bare.

Moments pause for thought and prayer,
In this sanctuary of peace.
Here the burdens lift, beware,
And all the world feels at ease.

As dawn paints the morning bright,
Hope awakens with the sun.
In this garden, pure delight,
Reflection of what we have done.

Nature's Palette

Dappled shades of green and gold,
Brushstrokes made by sun and rain.
Mountains high and valleys bold,
Nature sings her sweet refrain.

Every hue a story told,
In the petals, leaves, and sky.
Crimson sunsets, nights so cold,
In her canvas, wonders lie.

From the ocean's deep embrace,
To the heights of ancient trees,
Every corner holds a grace,
Nature whispers on the breeze.

Artistry in every glance,
Wonders crafted, wild and free.
In her arms, we find our chance,
To feel alive, to truly see.

Breezes of Change

Gentle winds through fields will roam,
Carrying whispers of the past.
Every gust can feel like home,
Yet swiftly, time's shadows cast.

Leaves will turn from green to gold,
Seasons shift in dance and sway.
Life unfolds like tales retold,
In each breath, a new bouquet.

With the storm, the voices rise,
Change can sometimes sting the heart.
Yet in struggle, hidden skies,
Promise of a brand new start.

Let the breezes guide your way,
Feel the warmth of morning light.
In the cycles, find your stay,
Embrace the change, ignite your flight.

The Spectrum of Sentiments

In gentle whispers, joy takes flight,
While shadows linger, dimming light.
A laughter shared, a tear released,
Emotions dance, in chaos, ceased.

Each heartbeat echoes love's refrain,
In tender moments, loss and gain.
The spectrum wide, like painted skies,
We find our truths in whispered lies.

A fleeting glance, a longing sigh,
In silence, dreams, both low and high.
The colors blend, a vivid hue,
Life's tender brush, it pierces through.

With every choice, a path unfolds,
From pale to rich, the heart beholds.
In every shade, a tale we weave,
The spectrum blooms, as we believe.

Dreamscapes in Blossom

In twilight's hush, where dreams take root,
The petals of the night, in pursuit.
A symphony of stars, they bloom,
Creating worlds, dispelling gloom.

With fragrant tales upon the breeze,
An echoing song of rustling trees.
Each dream a petal, soft and bright,
In gardens filled with silver light.

A canvas painted in gentle hues,
Where moonlit paths invite our views.
In whispers low, the nightingale sings,
As heartbeats dance on feathered wings.

In sleep's embrace, we wander free,
Through fields of hope, by the deep sea.
With every dawn, we find our grace,
In dreamscapes lush, we find our place.

Harvesting Hope

In fields of gold, where shadows play,
We gather dreams, come what may.
With gentle hands, we tend the seeds,
A bountiful weight, the heart's true needs.

The sun arises, casting glow,
With every trial, our spirits grow.
Through storms and droughts, we keep the faith,
Harvesting hope, with love as wraith.

Each grain a story, a tale to tell,
In fervent whispers, we break the spell.
As seasons change, we reap the yield,
In unity, our fate is sealed.

With every grain, a promise sown,
In fertile ground, our hearts have grown.
For hope's a crop, forever bloomed,
In every soul, its light consumed.

Whimsical Wanderings

Through forests deep, on winding trails,
Where laughter spills and wonder prevails.
The fluttering leaves, a dance of cheer,
In every step, the world draws near.

With twinkling eyes, we chase the light,
In corners strange, the wild delight.
A journey bright, by serendipity,
Where whimsical paths unfold with glee.

In meadows lush, where dreams take flight,
We twirl among the stars so bright.
With hearts unbound, our spirits rise,
In playful whispers, we touch the skies.

Embrace the road, the twists and bends,
In every turn, adventure blends.
For life's a dance, a wondrous waltz,
In whimsical wanderings, joy exalts.

Nature's Embrace

Whispers of the gentle breeze,
Softly cradling the trees.
Sunlight dances on the stream,
Nature's hug, a tender dream.

Mountains stand, a silent choir,
Echoing the sun's warm fire.
Clouds above in shades of white,
Nature's canvas, pure delight.

Fields adorned with blooms of gold,
Stories of the earth retold.
In this space where silence grows,
Beauty's breath forever flows.

Quiet moments, hearts align,
Nature's gift, a sacred sign.
In her arms, we find our place,
Lost in Nature's warm embrace.

Soulful Sprouts

From the soil, new life does rise,
Reaching up toward sunlit skies.
Each small sprout, a whispered chance,
In the soil, nature's dance.

Gentle rains, a nurturing touch,
Every drop means oh so much.
Rooted deep but reaching high,
Dreams of green in every sigh.

Petals bloom, their colors bright,
In the day and through the night.
Life unfolds in shades so true,
Soulful sprouts, a wondrous view.

Watch them grow, a tale untold,
Strength in moments, fierce and bold.
Nature sings, her voice so clear,
In the sprouts, hope draws near.

Ephemeral Impressions

Morning dew on blades of grass,
Moments fleeting, none will last.
Footsteps soft on paths unseen,
Evanescent, where we've been.

Winds of change, they softly blow,
Carrying seeds where dreams will grow.
Days drift by, like clouds they roam,
Impressions left, a heart finds home.

Colors fade, yet stories stay,
In the heart, we find our way.
Transient beauty all around,
In these moments, life is found.

Fleeting times, like whispered notes,
In the silence, wisdom floats.
Capture quick, embrace the now,
In impressions, we take a bow.

The Poetry of Greenery

Leaves like verses, fluttering free,
Nature writes in harmony.
Every branch, a story told,
In the green, a world unfolds.

Mossy carpets, soft and deep,
In their cradle, secrets keep.
Whispers of the forest fair,
Echoing in fragrant air.

Sun-drenched fields, a lyric bright,
In the day, a joy, a light.
Nature's prose, a gentle flow,
In her song, our hearts will grow.

Rustling leaves, a coded rhyme,
Nature's art transcends all time.
In every shade, each hue, each tone,
The poetry of green is sown.